# Be a Brilliant Dyslexic Student

T0021621

Sara Miller McCune founded SAGE Publishing in 1965 to support the dissemination of usable knowledge and educate a global community. SAGE publishes more than 1000 journals and over 800 new books each year, spanning a wide range of subject areas. Our growing selection of library products includes archives, data, case studies and video. SAGE remains majority owned by our founder and after her lifetime will become owned by a charitable trust that secures the company's continued independence.

Los Angeles | London | New Delhi | Singapore | Washington DC | Melbourne

SUPER
QUICK
SKILLS

# Be a Brilliant Dyslexic Student

Sarah J. Myhill

Los Angeles | London | New Delhi
Singapore | Washington DC | Melbourne

Los Angeles | London | New Delhi
Singapore | Washington DC | Melbourne

SAGE Publications Ltd
1 Oliver's Yard
55 City Road
London EC1Y 1SP

SAGE Publications Inc.
2455 Teller Road
Thousand Oaks, California 91320

SAGE Publications India Pvt Ltd
B 1/I 1 Mohan Cooperative Industrial Area
Mathura Road
New Delhi 110 044

SAGE Publications Asia-Pacific Pte Ltd
3 Church Street
#10-04 Samsung Hub
Singapore 049483

Editor: Jai Seaman
Editorial assistant: Hannah Cavender-Deere
Production editor: Victoria Nicholas
Marketing manager: Catherine Slinn
Cover design: Shaun Mercier
Typeset by: C&M Digitals (P) Ltd, Chennai, India
Printed in the UK

**Library of Congress Control Number: 2022933114**

**British Library Cataloguing in Publication data**

A catalogue record for this book is available from
the British Library

ISBN 978-1-5297-9081-8

At SAGE we take sustainability seriously. Most of our products are printed in the UK using responsibly
sourced papers and boards. When we print overseas we ensure sustainable papers are used as measured
by the PREPS grading system. We undertake an annual audit to monitor our sustainability.

**A message from the author about the book title**

We understand that many of you don't want to feel defined by your neuro-diversity, but also that it is a part of who you are and your life. After discussion with some of my students we chose this title for its positivity and empowering message. Ultimately this guide is to help you play to your strengths and be a brilliant student – with dyslexia.

# Contents

# Everything in this book!

### Section 5  My memory is not the best – how can I improve it?

Imagination + association = memory. A look at tried and tested strategies for improving memory to support academic work and revision skills.

### Section 6  How can mind mapping help me with my academic studies?

Mapping is a powerful way to support your planning, reading, assignments, note-taking, and revision. This section will show you how to understand and use mind maps more effectively.

### Section 7  How do I get my thoughts organized on paper?

An introduction to memorable approaches to planning and writing assignments. With tips to help with understanding and answering questions correctly and advice on how to make your written work flow more smoothly.

### Section 8  How can I improve my concentration?

Lack of concentration and focus is on the increase among students. This section will explore possible explanations and look at some solutions, including mindfulness and visualization.

### Section 9  How can I use my strengths for academic success?

Metacognition, or thinking about the way you think and learn best, can help you to start to use some of the strengths of dyslexia in order to work smart. You could ask a tutor, specialist support tutor, friend, or family member to go through the Activities in this book with you. They could be interesting and helpful to many people.

# What is dyslexia?
# How does it affect
# my academic studies?

10 second
summary

Dyslexia is mostly genetic in origin,
therefore inheritable and you don't
grow out of it. It results in difficulty
with specific areas of learning such
as reading, writing, spelling, working
memory, and the speed of processing
information. However, creative thinking
skills can be enhanced.

## Maybe you do learn differently – so play to your strengths

- Dyslexia is the most well-known and most frequently occurring learning difference.

- About 43% of students who have dyslexia are diagnosed when they reach university (National Working Party on Dyslexia, 1999; Singleton, 2004) and often not until their final year (Nichols et al., 2009).

- It has the most impact on your academic studies because it primarily affects the skills involved in accurate and fluent word reading and spelling.

- Verbal/short-term memory and verbal processing speeds can also be affected, skills which are used in learning.

- However, there are strategies to help alongside natural abilities in problem solving and creative thinking.

- Above all self-belief, motivation, and determination will be your greatest assets in helping you to reach your goals.

- Richard Macer in his documentary *Farther and Sun: A Dyslexic Road Trip* (2019), finds that some paleontologists think that the **leaders in prehistoric times** could well have been **dyslexic**.

- The **creative thinking and problem-solving skills** that are often strong in those with dyslexia may have led to the stone-tipped arrow and to fire, and therefore to admiration and leadership.

- Today, society chooses to judge ability by the written word but who is to say that is an accurate measure of intelligence.

- When asked, most employers value problem-solving skills over graduates with high grades but no **curiosity**.

- However, you do need to **find and reach your potential** and implementing some strategies can help you do this.

- It is thought that if dyslexia was not of benefit to the human race it would have died out long ago. **Today, more than ever, the strengths of dyslexia can shine because technology supports many of the difficulties,** with text-to-speech and speech-to-text facilities, which can really level the playing field at university.

- Neuro-imaging has been carried out on the brains of people with dyslexia and there appears to be a weakness in the area around the written word with a compensatory strength in the area of visual skills, creative thinking, and problem solving.

- Dyslexia is just one of a group of conditions under the umbrella term **neuro-diversity**.

- Neuro-diverse people can experience difficulties with organization, memory, concentration, time, direction, perception, and sequencing.

- They can have poor listening skills and concentration issues.

- These difficulties and issues may lead to low self-esteem, anxiety, and depression if others are not aware.

- BUT neuro-diverse people can also be creative, original, and determined.

- We may all be on the scale of neuro-diversity, in different areas and to greater and lesser extents.

Neuro-diversity
The view that any brain differences are normal and not deficits. Neuro-diverse people are unique in the way they interact with and interpret the world. The strengths of people with any learning difference are acknowledged and valued.

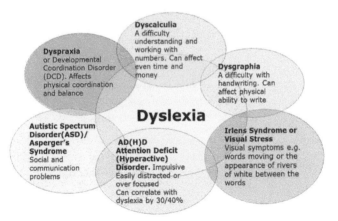

**Figure 1.1** These are just some of the learning differences than can overlap or 'correlate' with dyslexia or it can stand-alone

## Successful dyslexics

- 50% of entrepreneurs are dyslexic, including the billionaire Richard Branson. He claims that dyslexia is at least partially responsible for his success and that people with the condition are likely to have the skills necessary to excel in the future.

- Richard is involved in a great charity, Made by Dyslexia, filled with successful people and celebrities who feel they have been 'made by their dyslexia'!

- Albert Einstein, the famous physicist, was also dyslexic, so you're in good company.

- Dr Beryl Benacerraf (radiologist and expert in ultrasound of pregnancy) has said that she feels her brain works differently to others and she has a gift of seeing patterns in images that others don't see, which enhances her position in her job.

- Where would we be today without people like Richard Branson, Albert Einstein, and Dr Benacerraf?

> 'Everybody is a genius. But if you judge a fish by its ability to climb a tree, it will live its whole life believing that it is stupid.'
>
>  Albert Einstein (Connerr, 2016: 12)

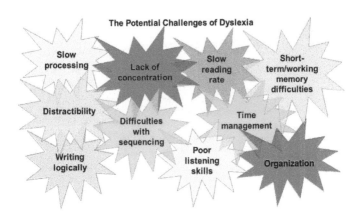

**Figure 1.2** Dyslexia is a learning difference with a combination of strengths and weaknesses that can impact your academic study

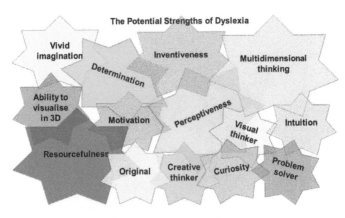

**Figure 1.3** The potential strengths of dyslexia

'I know that dyslexia should not be viewed as a
hindrance. In fact, I would not change it;
I like the fact that I think differently
to others.'

'Dyslexia is not a barrier to success; with support,
students can excel in their chosen course and
become a real asset to their university.'

# Check for potential dyslexic traits

Dyslexia will manifest differently in everyone but there are some common indicators so have a look at the checklist below and tick your combination.

| Area | How dyslexia might impact your academic learning | Tick if observed |
|---|---|---|
| Organization/ time management difficulties | • Hard to finish exams on time <br> • Can feel overwhelmed | |
| Procrastination/ emotional | • Avoid certain studies <br> • Hard to get started <br> • Get distracted easily | |
| Reading | • Slow reading pace <br> • Re-read texts <br> • Moving text | |
| Spelling | • Spell erratically <br> • Difficulty 'hearing' sounds | |
| Listening | • Note-taking a problem <br> • Background noise distracting | |
| Writing | • Difficulty structuring written work | |
| Memory difficulties | • Retaining and recalling information challenging | |
| Concentration difficulties | • Hard to listen and maintain focus | |
| Spatial/temporal | • Left right confusion <br> • Map reading difficult | |

| Area | How dyslexia might impact your academic learning | Tick if observed |
|---|---|---|
| **Number/maths difficulties** | • Mental maths challenging<br>• Time/money maths a problem | |
| **Motor control** | • Difficulty copying<br>• Handwriting and coordination difficult | |
| **Self confidence/ self esteem** | • Low self-esteem and confidence with work | |
| **Potential strengths** | • Good visualizing skills<br>• Good problem solver<br>• Good verbal ability | |

# I find organization and deadlines stressful – how can I manage my time better?

10 second
summary

The slow speed of processing information and short-term memory difficulties associated with dyslexia can result in problems with organization and time management but there are many tools to help.

60 second summary

## Time is our most precious resource

- It is important to manage time efficiently in order to study effectively.

- Being good at time management means organizing your time intentionally and not just drifting through life.

- It means prioritizing activities that efficiently move you towards your goals.

- To do this you need to get the 'big picture' of your life by analysing available time, your tasks, and your deadlines.

- Use calendars (online and on the wall), diaries, reminders, lists, post-its, and colour to highlight different subjects and tasks and arrange them effectively.

- Getting the 'big picture' allows your brain to see the boundaries and slot the detail in more quickly and efficiently.

# Why is time management important?

- You need to manage your time efficiently to study effectively and therefore increase your chances of employability and success in a competitive world. Effective time managers are often high achievers in life.

- When you start university it can seem as though you have so much free time with only a few hours of lectures/seminars a week and lots of time to yourself. Then, suddenly, your assignment deadline or your exams are the next week.

- Thinking about how you use your time and prioritize your activities could be the most valuable use of your time.

- It is easy to feel overwhelmed by the volume of work and tasks you need to achieve and the speed of life today, so minimize your stress and maximize success by becoming **proactive not reactive.** Take control of your life.

# Setting goals

Research has shown that those who set goals achieve more in life!

- **Where** do you want your studies to take you in life?

- **What** grades do you want to achieve? What is your ultimate goal?

- **When** do you want to achieve these goals? Lifetime, next five years, next year, next term, next week, tomorrow…?

- Set **achievable short-term goals** on the journey towards your **long-term goals.**

## Prioritize your tasks with

Eisenhower's Important/Urgent Matrix
time-management tool

- **Important** = an outcome that leads to achievement of your goals.

- **Urgent** = demands immediate attention; may be based on other people's priorities.

Decide whether a task is:

- **Important and urgent** (lectures, assignment deadlines, crises = **DO IT NOW**).

- **Important but not urgent** (preparing/planning, relaxation/exercise = **START BEFORE IT BECOMES URGENT = BUILDS SUCCESS**).

- **Urgent but not important** (interruptions, checking emails, Instagram?! = **DO IT IF YOU CAN/ AVOID**).

- **Not urgent or important** (trivia, junk mail, distractions = **DON'T DO IT**).

- You can use different coloured post-it notes on a larger grid that you fix to the wall and move about as your priorities change.

- Or, use a white board and coloured pens.

## Now

- Define your goals and priorities.

- Make a list of everything you need to do. Add anything else you usually do.

- Apply Eisenhower's Important/Urgent Matrix to prioritize your tasks – see the following Activity.

- Make a prioritized plan.

- Stick to your plan but allow for tweaks and flexibility.

A student told us

'Set yourself an individual deadline before the actual one. This will give you time to go back and check over things.'

Organize your to-do list

Organize your to-do list into your 'most/least' urgent and important tasks. Start working on the tasks in your urgent and important box first!

| URGENT AND IMPORTANT | IMPORTANT BUT NOT URGENT |
|---|---|
| URGENT BUT NOT IMPORTANT | NOT IMPORTANT AND NOT URGENT |

# CHECK POINT How to plan your time effectively

Keep the below tips in mind when approaching planning your work:

☐ **Identify time available and plan** what you can realistically achieve in this time.

☐ **Identify and use unproductive time** for other tasks.

☐ **Block in essential tasks.**

☐ **Reduce the number of tasks in a day** if you can. You are only likely to be able to achieve three or four main goals in a day.

☐ **Fill-in deadlines/urgent tasks** and work a timeline backwards from the deadline date.

☐ **Build in contingency** by imposing false deadlines, i.e., make a deadline the week before the real deadline.

☐ **Remember,** tasks always take longer than you expect and work tends to expand to fill the time available.

☐ **Tick off tasks by work completed** with less emphasis on how long they may take. A Results-Only Study Environment (ROSE) can increase productivity by as much as 41% (Tefula, 2012: 47).

☐ **Get the big picture or an overview** of your term or year by buying a large wall planner, it will keep you on track. Laptop and/or phone diaries and timetables are useful but you cannot see the big picture. Use highlighters and post-it notes to interact with your planner and keep it live!

☐ You can combine this with **more detailed timetables** so you can plan your time on a more micro-level (see example week planner on the next page). You could **divide your life into 21 sessions a week**: 7 days of morning, afternoon, and evening. Use a different colour for each module and block out lectures, tutorials, seminars, meetings, work, and social occasions – you'll then see what time is left free for study.

☐ You need to **plan in breaks too** – they help your recover and perform better.

☐ Build some **self-discipline** into your life; consider your most productive time of day and work in blocks of time with breaks.

☐ Use a **diary, Microsoft Outlook, or a planner** – weekly/daily as well, for when you are on the move, or carry a photo of your wall planner around!

☐ **Track progress** – remove completed tasks, carry over unfinished ones, re-prioritize.

☐ **Establish a routine.**

| WEEK | | 9am | 10am | 11am | 12.00 | 1pm | 2pm | 3pm | 4pm | 5pm | 6pm | 7pm | 8pm | 9pm |
|------|--|-----|------|------|-------|-----|-----|-----|-----|-----|-----|-----|-----|-----|
| MON 27/09 | | | | | | | | | | | | | | |
| TUES 28/09 | | | | | | | | | | | | | | |
| WED 29/09 | | | | | | Lunch | | | | | Dinner | | | |
| THUR 30/09 | | | | | | | | | | | | | | |
| FRI 01/10 | | | | | | | | | | | | | | |
| SAT 02/10 | | | | | | | | | | | | | | |
| SUN 03/10 | | | | | | | | | | | | | | |

**Figure 2.1** Example of 1 week from a planner divided into 21 sessions a week

## Time management tips using your mobile

- Remember you can synchronize your university Outlook email account to your phone calendar.

- Reminders: set alarms ahead of deadlines and appointments, maybe connect them to your calendar.

- Tasks: Use 'to-do' list facilities like: Todoist (linear) or Trello (visual).

- Timers: Can be useful for practising exam papers and using timed study methods. Try timer apps: Pomodoro Technique, Flora, or Focus.

- The Forest app grows trees while you study to help you stay focused and in the present.

'Time management should be a core skill around
which the rest of your life revolves.'

# How do I deal with procrastination?

10 second
summary

We all procrastinate, but when you have dyslexia reading and writing can take longer and require more effort, which can make getting started even harder. Understanding why you procrastinate and implementing strategies can help.

## Academic procrastination

- Psychological science reveals that procrastination undermines our performance, reduces well-being, harms work relationships, and correlates to poorer health, even coronary heart disease and hypertension (Ferrari et al., 2005 and Sirois et al., 2003).

- Studies have found a consistent rise in procrastination in the last four-decades among the population in general but the largest procrastinators have been found to be students (90%) (Svartdal and Steel, 2017).

- Academic procrastination can be fuelled by a lack of belief in one's own capabilities to carry out a specific task, such as completing an assignment.

- In students with dyslexia – this can be overlaid by lack of self-esteem and confidence arising from difficulties with schoolwork, especially if dyslexia has not been identified or supported as a child.

- Raising self-confidence and increasing motivation can go a long way to help; getting started and successfully completing one task can build motivation for more.

## What influences academic procrastination?

- **Self-efficacy**: The belief that you are capable of carrying out a specific task or of reaching a specific goal. Low self-efficacy was a strong predictor of procrastination in students (Steel, 2007).

- **Motivation** the force that drives a person to do something (de Charms, 1968).

- It can be intrinsic, such as feelings of gratification, or extrinsic, such as rewards (Ryan and Deci, 2000).

> **Academic procrastination** Students who put off academic work which they know they should be starting (Tefula, 2014).

- Intrinsically motivated students procrastinated less than extrinsically motivated students when performing the same task (Senécal et al., 1995).

- **Perfectionism** can cause students to adhere to strict and high standards for themselves and be severely self-critical. They are often high achievers but a fear of failure may cause them to procrastinate.

## Academic procrastination can result in

**Poor cognitive outcome**: Students have difficulties that arise from procrastination, such as ineffective learning skills, irrational thinking, and ineffective time management, which all adversely affect performance at university (Rozental and Carlbring, 2013). Procrastinators received lower marks on all their assignments (Tice and Baumeister, 1997).

**Poor psychological outcome**: Procrastinators experienced increased psychological distress and anxiety as deadlines approach due to fear of failing and low perceived self-ability (Balkis and Duru, 2007).

**Poor physical health outcome**: Procrastinators who completed their assignments later than non-procrastinators, experienced more stress and reported poor health symptoms, such as colds and flu (Abbasi and Alghamdi, 2015).

**Poor emotional outcome**: Procrastinators reported lower positive actions and more negative emotions than non-procrastinators (Ferrari and Díaz-Morales, 2014).

**Poor economic outcome**: Procrastinators showed less commitment and poor willingness in job search behaviours after graduating (Gupta et al., 2012).

From *A Study of Academic Procrastination* by Saman Awan (2018).

## Procrastination is an emotion management problem

- If we have negative emotions about a task we avoid it but it is a short-term solution and the task does not go away.

- **Guilt and shame** are some of the most common emotions associated with procrastination.

- **Emotion regulation** can decrease procrastination and these skills can be learned.

- **Awareness, understanding, acceptance/tolerance, coping ability, and the ability to modify emotional experience** are all emotion regulating skills.

A student told us

'Everything doesn't need to be done in one sitting or even 10. Making a start can be writing 30 words, but this could give you the motivation you need.'

Reflect on your task

What emotions do you feel are linked to the task?

..........................................................................................

..........................................................................................

..........................................................................................

..........................................................................................

Is it the right task/goal for now?

..........................................................................................

..........................................................................................

..........................................................................................

..........................................................................................

Do you really want to achieve this task/goal?

..........................................................................................

..........................................................................................

..........................................................................................

..........................................................................................

Is it a step towards a long-term goal?

..........................................................................................

..........................................................................................

..........................................................................................

..........................................................................................

What are the advantages of your procrastination?

...............................................................................

...............................................................................

...............................................................................

...............................................................................

What are the disadvantages of your procrastination?

...............................................................................

...............................................................................

...............................................................................

...............................................................................

A sense of commitment and excitement means you have the right
goals. Do you have this sense about your goals?

...............................................................................

...............................................................................

...............................................................................

...............................................................................

# CHECK POINT — Why do you procrastinate?

Try to recognize why you procrastinate; reflect on the reasons below and tick off any that might apply to you.

☐ Lack of self-belief in carrying out a specific task

☐ Poor organizational or decision-making skills

☐ Perfectionism

☐ Fear of failure/feeling overwhelmed/anxiety

☐ Negative emotions

☐ Talking rather than doing, over-planning

☐ Not managing interruptions

☐ External or self-induced distractions? (Frequent switching between tasks wastes time)

# Strategies to help beat academic procrastination

## Self-efficacy

- **Positive self-talk:** Prevents ego depletion and promotes self-belief.

- **Success breeds success** so build on feelings of accomplishment.

- **Mindset**: Imagine yourself doing the task and finishing the task.

- **Give yourself credit.** Highly successful and productive people give themselves credit. Procrastinators tend to do just the opposite.

## Motivation

- **Don't wait for motivation** or to be in the right mood – just act!

- **ACTION → MOTIVATION → MORE ACTION.**

- **Activity often breeds more activity**; action comes first and motivation comes second.

**Self-talk** Short sentences repeated internally or externally until your brain starts to believe them and then works towards that outcome (Knight, 2019). Self-talk is also a form of concentration training because you have to focus on the words. It changes your mindset and identity.

**Mindset** How you set your mind and your beliefs. Students with a 'growth' mindset (Dweck, 2006), who believe that the brain can grow and change with learning, tend to perform better than students with a 'fixed' mindset. Thinking about a task before you do it can get you in the right mindset and make the task easier.

- **Completing a project** builds more confidence and motivation to do it again.

- **List everything you've achieved in a day.**

- **Find something interesting** in your work.

## Perfectionism

- **Lower your standards a little**; perfectionism and fear of failure can paralyse you.

- **Be more relaxed** to be more creative and more productive.

- **Identify** your fear.

- **Failure is a stepping stone to success** and a necessary human learning tool.

## Performance

- Inhibit multi-tasking.

- Break up tasks into small, manageable units, and link study to small rewards so that studying becomes a positive experience.

- Consider your working environment: How and where do you work best? Declutter!

- Reduce the number of tasks.

- Work in short spurts with breaks – use a timer.

- Make a plan. Include timings. Tell someone else when you are going to start to validate it.

- Very specific intentions in the form of 'when …then' make a big difference to success.

## Finally

Try asking 'how' am I procrastinating instead of 'why'?

- When you ask: How can I move forward? How can I stop procrastinating? How can I do this? The mind starts to think about 'how' it can get a desired outcome.

- **'Why' stops you seeing the solutions.**

- **'How' questions make your brain search for solutions** and try to achieve those outcomes.

- Ask 'how' regularly and frequently and see what changes over time?

(Adapted from *How to…* blog by Kam Knight (2019b))

'Procrastination is the thief of time.'

# I read more slowly than my peers – what can I do?

10 second
summary

Students with dyslexia often have a slow reading rate and re-read text many times in order to absorb the information. Reading strategies and techniques can really improve this.

## Use your brain as well as your eyes to read!

- If you can **build an overall picture** of what you are studying **before you start reading** from beginning to end, you can form a map in your mind and see how the details fit together more easily.

- Getting a **preview** or big picture of a book **allows your brain to see** how the details connect and **where and what you need to study –** you might not even need to read chapters 8 and 9 to answer your assignment question!

- **Try the 80/20 technique**: it's based on a business model, where it is said 80% of your custom comes from 20% of your customers. It is possible to gain 80% of the meaning from a book or article by reading 20% of it.

- It is better to go through a book, an article, or lecture slides **3–4 times more quickly than once slowly**, it holds your attention and is more fun!

# Read a book like a jigsaw

- In the analogy with a jigsaw puzzle, you would first look at the picture on the box lid to get a preview of the puzzle. It would be hard to complete without doing this.

- Likewise get a 'preview' of your book or article – skim through it from cover to cover. Getting a preview of any reading material will help you to read it more quickly.

- With the puzzle you would then look for the corner pieces and the straight edges and start to fill-in the rest.

- You can read a book like this – this section will tell you more.

**Figure 4.1**   Read a book like a jigsaw

1. **Preview** – get the 'big picture', like the jigsaw box lid. Flick through the book, article, or lecture slides just getting the boundaries of the information.

2. **Read the introduction** and go straight to the **conclusion** or summary.

3. **Look at the diagrams, graphs, contents, chapter headings, and index.** If you can highlight in one colour all the chapter headings and sub-headings (it helps to break up the text) and read them aloud, this is like putting the corner pieces of your jigsaw in place.

4. Then **highlight the first sentence of every paragraph** in another colour which should tell you the topic/subject of that paragraph (don't read any more than that for now) and read them aloud. You are putting the straight edges of your jigsaw in place.

5. Then **look for more detail** where/if/when you need it, like filling in the jigsaw!

6. So, **you have gone through the book/ article/lecture slides four times without reading in detail yet but you have a very good idea about the contents**, layout, and where you need to focus your reading. It will therefore be easier to pick out the core messages and slot in the details.

**Big picture** Getting the big picture is to briefly look at the whole of the information in front of you, e.g., book, article, lecture slides, and see the extent of it to the boundaries. It helps you to identify the main points and to slot-in the detail more easily to the whole.

**Preview** Similar to getting the big picture; skim and scan something quickly before looking at it more closely. You can identify how the parts fit together then and what you need to concentrate on.

## Five minute jotter

- Spend five minutes jotting down everything you know about the subject before starting reading.

- This establishes your mindset which makes tasks easier.

- New knowledge hooks onto old knowledge much more easily than starting fresh.

## Set goals and objectives

- Why am I reading this?

- What do I want to get out of this?

- For a journey you would set a destination and use a route map: do the same when reading a book or article to help identify what you need to read.

## Keywords and key themes

- **Think about keywords and key themes:** the brain will start to look for the words in the text.

## Read actively

- **Write notes** in the margins or a notebook, either summaries or thoughts that could be used in an essay later. Even if you don't look at the notes again the **kinaesthetic action** between your hand and your brain **helps you to remember** the information.

## Use a guide

- A pencil, chopstick, or finger will anchor your eyes and help you to read more smoothly.

A student told us

'If possible, try and use text-to-speech software because hearing it while you're reading will help you to retain it in your memory.'

# Chunk your time

1. **Set a time period before commencing any study,** for instance 2 to 3 hours, and decide how much you would like to cover in this time period. Research suggests that the human brain has a very strong tendency to complete things when it knows the boundaries.

   > Chunking time
   > Breaking study time into 25–40 minute study sessions with a 5–10 minute break before starting the next period of study. The breaks are as important as the study sessions.

2. **Set a timer for a period of say 25 to 40 minutes.** When the timer goes off stop and take a break. Set a timer for your break of 5 to 10 minutes and go and do something different – **only for 5 to 10 minutes though!**

3. **When you return to your study, briefly look over or 'review' what you have just read** as this helps to embed the memory and reinforces what you have just learned. Have a quick look over what you are about to study and then start another period of 25 to 40 minutes (setting a timer).

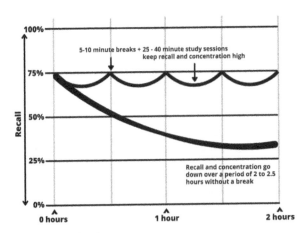

**Figure 4.2** Chunking time

4. Have another **5 to 10 minute break.** When you come back skim over or 'review' the last two study sessions that you have completed. Complete the overall amount of time that you decided on at the beginning if you can.

## Beginnings and endings

- The **beginnings and endings of anything studied tend to be remembered more than information covered in the middle.** The more beginnings and endings you have, the more likely you are to commit information to memory.

## Recall and concentration

- **This way of studying also keeps recall and concentration high**. Working for two and a half hours straight means that recall and concentration tend to drop dramatically during that time.

**Recall** Retrieval or recall deals with getting the information out of the mind and is one of the best ways to reinforce memory. The more you practice retrieval the more it motivates your mind to commit new information to memory.

## Breaks

- The **breaks themselves are just as important as the study periods** because they give the brain a chance to absorb the information and to integrate with previous information learned.

## Review

- **Review is as important as preview** (or getting the 'big picture').

- **80% of detail is forgotten within 24 hours so you need to review** a book, study period, set of lecture slides, lecture, or tutorial **within 24 hours** to help embed the information.

**Review** In this context, review is to skim or look back over a book, study period, lecture slides, a lecture, or tutorial to help to embed the information.

- **Skim or look over it quickly** for **10 minutes on day 2, 5 minutes on day 7,** and **2 to 4 minutes on day 30** (see Figure 4.3 below).

- This way, **the information will stay fresh in your mind** and you will not have a huge mountain of revision to climb when you come to the exams.

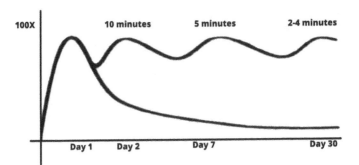

**Figure 4.3**  Review

Adapted from Knight, 2016

- **Review** is an excellent return on investment. Five minutes can potentially save you hours of time when you come to the exams (Knight, 2016).

> 'Use "preview" and "review" in all your academic work.'

**CHECK POINT** Remember how these strategies help with reading and studying?

Tick them off if you do or revisit the section if not.

☐ Preview: read a book like a jigsaw with the 80/20 technique

☐ Five minute jotter

☐ Set goals and objectives

☐ Keywords and key themes

☐ Read actively

☐ Use a guide

☐ Chunk your time

☐ Beginnings and ends

☐ Recall and concentration

☐ Breaks

☐ Review

# Congratulations!

You have learnt what dyslexia is, how it can impact your academic performance, and that it is not a barrier to academic success! You have also learnt how managing your time and setting priorities is key to that success. Techniques to help overcome procrastinating when starting tasks have been discussed as well as some study and reading strategies that have helped fellow students absorb more, faster!

# My memory is not the best – how can I improve it?

10 second
summary

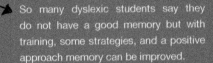

So many dyslexic students say they do not have a good memory but with training, some strategies, and a positive approach memory can be improved.

## Your memory is better than you think; it just needs some training

- Verbal memory is our ability to remember language-based information. We use both our visual and verbal memories to help us remember information.

- If you were to see somebody dressed in purple walking down the street, you are far more likely to remember them than all the other people in ordinary clothes.

- If you want to remember information you need to use your imagination to make it more memorable.

- When you link or associate information to other pieces of information, for instance, places, smells, people, and sounds, you're using your senses to embed the memory.

# Different types of memory

It is worth knowing that there are different types of memory because once you are aware of this you can use the different characteristics to help you remember more! There are also other types of memory besides these ones.

| Type of memory | What it does | How it relates to learning |
|---|---|---|
| **Episodic memory** | Memory of recent experiences personal to you, e.g., what you had for lunch, what you wore to work. | These associations are good for remembering if you can link learning to place (where you heard it), circumstance (who told you, what they were wearing, what happened) and incorporate senses too. |
| **Semantic memory** | A category of long-term memory that involves the recollection of ideas, concepts, and facts commonly regarded as general knowledge. | Underpins learning. It is to do with the meaning of words and putting them into context based on what you already know. Link new learning to old learning or to events outside your university life and studies. |
| **Sequential memory** | The ability to perceive and remember information in the right order, e.g., months of the year, the alphabet. | Sequential memory can be a problem for people with dyslexia. Can help with memorising, in terms of linking information. |

| Short-term memory | Involves repeating information over and over to help you remember. | You don't do anything with the information, for instance phone numbers, lists, rote learning. |
|---|---|---|
| Working memory | Requires you to apply or do something with the information that is sitting in your short-term memory, before it slips away or is stored. | Holding and manipulating information to make meaning out of it, e.g., mental maths. |
| Verbal working memory | Is used to remember oral instructions. | Learning of new words. Performing comprehension tasks. Writing essays when free writing. Taking notes. |
| Visuo-spatial working memory | Is used to remember sequences of events, patterns, and images. | This type of memory can be strong in people with dyslexia. Maths skills. Visual tasks and designs. Creative thinking. Problem solving. |

Memory checker

Look at these words for 1 minute (60 secs) then cover them and see how many you can remember – write in the space on the next page.

| kitten | toaster | and | far |
|--------|---------|-----|-----|
| was | Richard Branson | the | leg |
| soft | at | far | and |
| right | raft | leg | to |
| two | lunch | and | very |
| much | room | to | same |
| mother | it | very | finger |
| left | and | same | nail |
| it | the | the | as |
| cake | love | kitchen | birthday |

## How did you approach this task?

It sounds obvious but paying attention/concentrating/being interested at the time we learn/hear something is so important! Did you apply concentration to this task?

Tick the words you remembered

| Kitten and birthday? | We tend to remember information at beginnings and ends more than middles. | |
|---|---|---|
| Richard Branson? | His name stands out.<br>We remember situations, people, and information that stands out to us. **The more memorable something is the more you will remember it.**<br>**More extraordinary = more memorable.** | |
| Finger and nail? | We use our existing knowledge to chunk familiar information together. New learning or new memories link onto old learning. | |
| Kitchen and toaster? | We make associations and links to remember. Where did you eat your lunch? What room was the lecture in? What was the tutor wearing? | |
| Mother and cake? | We remember personal memories. | |
| And, the, to, very? | Repeated words. | |
| Love and soft? | We also use our senses to aid memory. A multisensory approach (using lots of your senses) helps. Music, smell, sound, and touch can bring back a memory. Reading something, hearing it read to you, repeating it out loud, and writing notes helps to embed a memory. | |

A student told us

'It sounds cliché but you can improve your memory just by adopting a healthier diet, a good sleeping pattern, and taking more exercise.'

## Other memory techniques

### Mnemonics

- **Stimulate your imagination** to encourage your brain to make associations.

- **Sentence/rhyme**: Necessary – it is necessary for a shirt to have one collar and two sleeves to remind you that there is one c and two s's in the word necessary.

- **Acronyms**: e.g., HOMES = Great Lakes – Huron, Ontario, Michigan, Erie, and Superior.

- **Memory palaces** or **Roman rooms/routes technique**: This stimulates your memory by linking something you know, for example, the rooms in your home or a familiar route, to information you are trying to remember, such as a module for an exam. For instance, the main topic could be linked in your imagination to the kitchen table, the chairs around the table to the core themes, the toaster or the kettle to other pieces of information. The same with a familiar route: a gate is linked to an introductory theme and items along the route to other information you want to remember.

### Self-quizzing and spaced-out retrieval

- Use **self-quizzing** with low level questions, such as: What are the key ideas? What terms or ideas are new to me? How would I define them? How did the ideas relate to what I already know?

- **Space out** (leave a day or two) between your study sessions so that a little forgetting has happened since your last practice, then come back and answer those questions and retrieve from your memory.

- **Retrieval** deals with getting the information out and reinforces memories.

- **Interleave** the subjects you are revising.

## Make learning more fun to remember more

- **Teach others**: Teach your study to colleagues, members of the family, a pet, or the mirror!

- **Playing academic Trivial Pursuit or Pairs**: Select keywords, ideas, or concepts and copy them onto blank business cards (available online). Put keywords on one card and the explanation on another. Then play with a buddy, a group, or on your own.

- **Rhythm/melody**: For those who are musical and can remember/enjoy melodic lines or long lyrical sequences, matching this with revision can work.

## Last but not least

- Making mental visual images can help you to remember.

- Mind maps help with memory by linking keywords to key images.

- Preview to get the big picture.

**Visualization** Link words to images in your mind to remember more. We are visual beings so we can use our imagination to create mental pictures to help embed memories.

**Mind mapping** A diagrammatic, visual way of portraying and analysing information using trigger words and images that encourage the left and right sides of the brain to work together to reinforce memories. Useful for planning, taking/making notes, and revision, etc. Shows the big picture and how ideas are connected. Clarifies thinking and simplifies complex ideas. An effective memory tool. Encourages creative thinking, which promotes more ideas.

- Use repetition in different ways. Build up layers of repetition.

- Taking breaks: Your brain is like a muscle and breaks aid performance.

- Summaries consolidate memories and core points.

- Condense down your notes to identify key or recall words and core themes, which is useful for revision.

> 'Sleep is necessary to transfer short-term memories into long term memory, which is what is needed for study and to pass exams!'

# How can mind mapping help me with my academic studies?

10 second
summary

Many students have heard of mind mapping but do not know how useful it can be for brainstorming ideas and organizing thoughts. It's a creative tool that can work well with the dyslexic brain.

60 second
summary

## Mind maps can support an increase in academic performance

### Mind maps

- Are a visual way of taking/making notes and planning.

- Show the big picture and how ideas are connected.

- Clarify thinking and simplify complex ideas.

- Encourage creative thinking, which equals more ideas.

- Are an effective way to improve learning and memory because they're compatible with the way our brains function.

- Mirror the way we think in multiple directions simultaneously from central trigger points in keywords and key images, rather than in a linear way.

- Link words to images, which therefore works the left and right brain together and helps to embed information more securely in our memory.

- Align with our tendency to think in images rather than words.

# A picture paints a thousand words

- Mind maps have been devised to use our natural preference for thinking in pictures.

- Students with dyslexia can also have a preference for non-linear thought and think in multiple directions simultaneously, just like a mind map, starting from central trigger points in keywords and key images.

- A keyword is a memory trigger and when linked to a key image can stimulate both wordy left and visual right sides of the brain and involve your senses.

- This helps to embed information into your memory.

- Keywords make links that trigger recall of complete associated information.

- The result is an increase in your performance.

# Hand-drawn or online mind maps?

Both mapping styles have a place in supporting academic studies.

## Hand-drawn mind maps

- Encourage a free flow of thoughts onto the paper.

- Promote a kinaesthetic action between your hand and brain, which helps with memorizing.

- Are restricted by the edge of the paper.

- Are good for revision.

## Online maps

- Can be as large as you like. Pre-set symbols are available to use.

- Making changes is much easier.

- You can put a lot more information on the map.

- Automatically attaches references to images and texts from the internet.

- Are great for analysing and understanding systems and processes. Are not as interactive as hand drawn maps.

- Information is separated from other information by a single line, with no linking words, therefore reducing the flow of thought outwards from the central image.

- Some software can be quite expensive but there are many good free or inexpensive software packages out there.

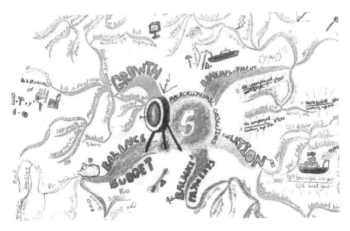

**Figure 6.1** Student hand-drawn mind map

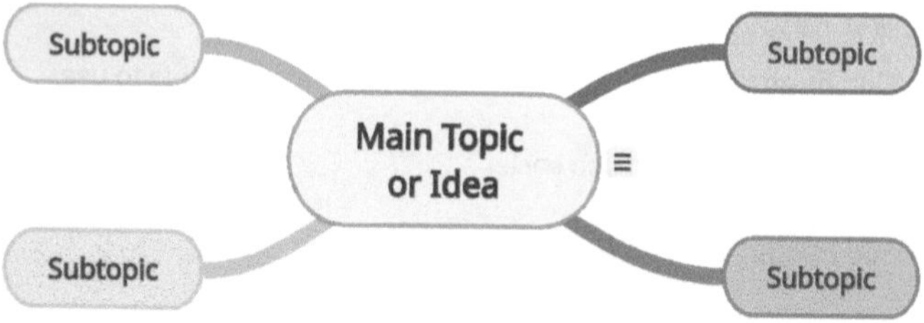

**Figure 6.2** Example of online mind map

## How to create a hand drawn mind map

- **Reduce your notes** or information **to one keyword or** pull out a **recall word** (a word that triggers the text that it is related to).

- **Try to use keywords on the main branches rather than key phrases** which can be limiting.

- Start your map with a **strong central positive image** to anchor it in your memory and differentiate it from your other maps. You don't want to mix up your mind maps when you come to the exams!

- Make sure your **main branches attach to the central image.**

- To aid memory, write the **keywords in capitals on the line** or in the line.

- Your **branches should be curved**: the human brain responds better to curved lines than straight lines.

- The brain is also **stimulated by the use of colour**, so use as many different colours as possible on your mind map.

- If you can't think of an image, **decorate the word to make it memorable**.

- Use **word bubbles** or **branch clouds**; see examples on the next page.

**Figure 6.3** Examples of mind map words

The reason for these strict instructions is to make
a map that:

- **Encourages the flow of thought** out from the central image to the main branches and related ones.

- **Creates the links** that are going to help you remember that map in an exam.

- **Makes associations** between your ideas.

- **Helps you understand the subject** at a deeper level

- Helps you to **organize and clarify your thoughts**.

Learning to mind map is like learning to drive a car, you need to **practise, practise, and practise to be proficient!**

**Mind maps** are a unique tool for **aiding recall** and helping **organize thoughts** to **make connections**. They allow you to associate your think-ing, which is essential for triggering related memories.

**ACTIVITY** Create a mind map of your strengths

Include, in particular, strengths that are related to academic work.

Think about what makes you 'feel' strong too!

Could any of those strengths be used to overcome anything you find more difficult?

A student
told us

'In academic study you will always need to make connections between different ideas and mind mapping can help you discover these connections.'

## Other uses of mind maps

**Note-taking:** Create a map before a lecture and add to it during the lecture.

**Note-making:** Make a map of the main themes in the book/article/lecture you are studying and add related branches. You will be able to make more connections.

**Revision**: Create a hand drawn map using the method above as a memory aid.

**Planning assignments:** Get an overview of your assignment and plan your paragraphs with a hand drawn or online map.

## Other kinds of maps

Different forms of map are defined by:

- The relationships they depict.

- What goes in the boxes.

- What the connecting lines mean.

## Argument mapping

- Argument maps are driven by the question: **Why should I believe that?**

- The lines mean something very specific: **a reason to 'believe' or a reason 'not to believe'** an argument.

- They **allow you to tease apart an argument** and reduce it to its core components.

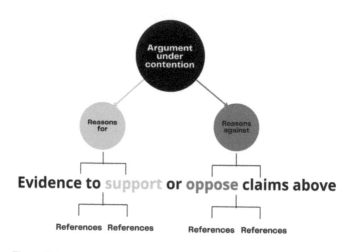

**Figure 6.4**  Argument map format

## Concept maps

- Provide meaning as to how ideas connect.

- The lines show how pieces of information relate.

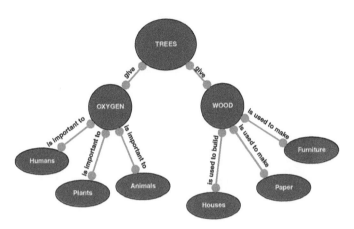

**Figure 6.5** Concept map format

There are other diagrams, such as **flow diagrams**, that allow you to analyse systems and processes. Search for other styles of maps and diagrams that might suit your purpose.

> 'Use mapping and diagrams to make the most of a dyslexic tendency to see connections.'

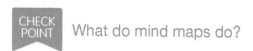

What do mind maps do?

Tick if you remember how they do it.

☐ Support planning and note-taking

☐ Support revision

☐ Improve memory

☐ Improve recall

☐ Improve the power of association to remember more

☐ Encourage connections to be made

# How do I get my thoughts organized on paper?

10 second
summary

Many dyslexic students have great verbal skills but find writing information down in a logical format much more difficult. Using a structure and visual approaches can help overcome this barrier.

60 second
summary

## Visual skills and 'big picture' planning support academic writing

- Getting the big picture can help with writing.

- Build assignments and essays in a more global way rather than starting at the beginning and finishing at the end as in a linear format.

- Use a mind map to brainstorm ideas and see connections.

- Then transfer the ideas onto an 'essay planner' where paragraph 5 might be written before paragraph 1.

- Each paragraph should be about a topic so use this structure to cluster ideas under topics before starting to write.

- Critical thinking is important and a valuable skill to develop further while at university because it is where the higher marks are, and it is a skill that students with dyslexia can be particularly good at.

## Not answering the question

- It sounds too simple but one of the top reasons for students not achieving well in assignments or exams is that they didn't answer the question correctly.

## HUG method of answering a question:

**H**ighlight the action word (verb).

**U**nderscore important information.

**G**o back over the question again.

**Example:** <u>Electric lighting</u> impacted <u>architectural design</u> hugely when it came into use in the <u>late 1870s</u>, however, the <u>science</u> of artificial lighting <u>advanced far more rapidly than</u> it did as a <u>design medium</u>. Critically analyse.

## Commonly used action words (verbs) in academic questions are often instruction words

| Action word (verb) | What it means |
|---|---|
| Analyse | Assess and identify strengths/weaknesses/flaws |
| Compare/contrast | Identify similarities and differences |
| Criticise | Explore strengths/weaknesses/flaws in depth |
| Describe | Identify and outline key characteristics |
| Evaluate | Judge the pros and cons from evidence available |
| Explain | Give reasons or purposes for something |
| Outline | Identify and describe the main characteristics |
| Summarize | Identify/describe the main points without detail |

# Planning your assignment: Get the 'big picture'

- **Brainstorm** all your ideas onto a piece of A3 paper if possible or onto a Word document.

- Use different coloured highlighters to **link related information** that you would like to put into various paragraphs.

- Use a **mind map** to collect your ideas together.

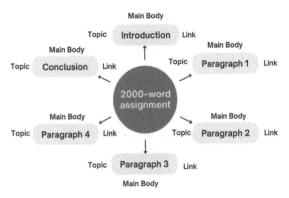

**Figure 7.1**   Structure of a 2000-word assignment

- Bullet point your ideas.

- Use an essay planner to plan your assignment in a big picture rather than a linear way (where you start at the beginning and finish at the end).

- Write your assignment title in the middle of the page so that your writing is relevant.

- Make a 2000-word assignment less intimidating by taking out 10% of the word count for the introduction and 10% for the conclusion – don't even write them immediately – you can leave them to the end if you wish.

- You then have 1600 words to distribute between 4/5 or more paragraphs.

## ACTIVITY Plan out your assignment

Use the essay planner template below. Distribute the word count across the different sections and use the PEAL structure (see page 88) to plan out each paragraph.

| Introduction (10%) | Total word count | Conclusion (10%) |
|---|---|---|
| | | |
| | **For example**: 2000-word essay | |
| | 3, 4 or more paragraphs | |
| | **Intro**: 200 words | |
| | **Concl**: 200 words | |
| | **4 paragraphs**: 400 words each | |
| | **P**oint being made; topic sentence | |
| | **E**xample, demonstrate point | |
| | **A**nalysis of above | |
| | **L**ink to title/point/next paragraph | |

| Paragraph 1 | Essay title | Paragraph 5 |
| --- | --- | --- |
| | Write here and keep checking back | |

| Paragraph 2 | Paragraph 3 | Paragraph 4 |
| --- | --- | --- |
| | | |

# Writing your assignment: Structure, structure, structure

A logical, coherent structure is a good basis for effective academic writing.

## Paragraphs

Each paragraph should be about a subject or topic.

PEAL your paragraph structure:

**P**oint or topic you are trying to discuss

**E**xample or evidence for your point

**A**nalysis of the topic (this is where the marks are!)

**L**ink back to the title or the next paragraph.

## Sentences

A simple sentence structure could **start with your subject or topic** and then be followed by an **action word** and then the **details/specifics.**

SAD will help your sentences flow better:

**S**ubject/topic/noun followed by an

**A**ction word/verb followed by

**D**etails/specifics/descriptive words

**Example:** Electric lighting (**subject/topic/noun**) impacted (**action word/verb**) architectural design hugely when it came into use in the late 1870s (**details**).

A student told us

> 'I got mediocre marks until I realized that I was not putting enough critical analysis into my assignments; when I did I started getting firsts!'

## Don't just lay the table, add food and drink

- Another common reason for students not doing well in assignments or exams is that there is **too much description** (breadth) and **not enough critical analysis** (depth).

- Don't just **lay the table** with your writing (description) and get mediocre marks; make sure you actually **put food on the plates** (add critical analysis and your own voice)!

- **Critical thinking tip!** Consider: **What, why, when, how, where** in your writing.

- Critical thinking analysis can be very **compatible with dyslexic thinking.** It can be an area where **students with dyslexia can excel** and it is where the potential for the most marks is concentrated in an assignment.

- Ask yourself – '**so what?**' at the end of each paragraph. Is what you said in that paragraph relevant to your writing and to your argument?

## Check the balance of your argument

- Academic writing is characterized by its critical elements and, as mentioned previously, this is where many of the marks can be gained.

- Assess your written assignment for critical, analytical content using different coloured highlights online or on paper.

- Highlight different sides of the argument using different colours.

- You could then use a third colour for your own opinion, your own voice, having weighed up the evidence.

- Use different coloured pens in the margins to note descriptive and critical sections of the text. You can then see if you have enough of the critical element.

## Proofreading

- It can be very difficult for students with dyslexia to see the mistakes in their writing.

- Reading out loud to someone else or to the mirror can be helpful in spotting those errors as they are easier to hear than see.

- Speech-to-text software is also very good these days and is embedded into software such as Word online – see Next Steps at the end of the book.

# General tip for the dyslexic student

- It is not very environmentally friendly but it can really help to **print your reading and writing out** if possible.

- **Viewing things on paper** is better for students with dyslexia than scrolling on a computer screen.

These are just some tips to help dyslexic students with structuring their words on paper. There are also many good books by SAGE in this SQS Series with more detailed information to help you with writing your assignments and essays, such as *Think critically* (Chatfield, 2019), *Build your argument* (Rush, 2020) and *Plan your essay* (Shon, 2019).

> 'When you apply some structure to your writing you will find that it will flow more easily.'

**CHECK POINT** Can you remember what the acronyms mean? Fill in the boxes:

**HUG** your answer

| H | |
|---|---|
| U | |
| G | . |

**PEAL** your paragraph

| P | |
|---|---|
| E | |
| A | |
| L | |

**SAD** will help sentence structure

| S | |
|---|---|
| A | |
| D | |

# Congratulations!

You have learned a little about how we remember, using imagination and association, and how you can use some tried and tested strategies to help you remember more. You have also learned how mapping can help with thinking and planning for assignments in a visual way and how structuring written work will help thoughts to flow better on paper. Just being aware of these techniques and employing some of them to study more effectively can really improve academic performance.

# How can I improve my concentration?

10 second
summary

There are many demands on our attention these days, especially from technology. Recognizing this and implementing some concentration techniques can help dyslexic students to focus.

## Concentration is key to academic success

- We can find it hard to concentrate because there are so many thoughts invading our minds and so many distractions these days.

- We have become so used to attending immediately to these distractions, such as text messages and social media posts, that we have worn down our attention spans.

- We need to become aware of this and build up our concentration 'will' again.

- You can do this by becoming aware of the impact of thoughts and emotions on your concentration and using techniques like **positive self-talk, visualization, concentration exercises,** and **mindfulness exercises** to promote concentration.

- And last but not least **lifestyle choices have a huge impact on your concentration** and academic achievement, so make healthy choices for peak performance.

# Improve your focus to improve your grades

- 'Concentration is the ability to focus your attention on a single thought, idea, or action, as critical as this skill is, it is one of the most difficult to develop' (Knight, 2019a: 1).

- Concentration is a critical skill for a student, without it, you are not able to start, stick with, or finish a task or an assignment (Knight, 2019a).

- Mindfulness can strengthen the focus area of your brain and therefore raise your grades.

- Students with dyslexia often suffer with lack of concentration but they can often work more intensely than other students between distracted periods!

> Mindfulness The art of being able to distance yourself from your thoughts and let them move by without being affected by them. It is a form of brain training and can help focus, which can then improve your grades and reduce anxiety. To develop mindfulness takes practice and persistence but can have big rewards.

- Short rests/naps can help to re-balance and re-set concentration.

- Don't compare yourself with others because you have a unique learning strategy.

- Check your lifestyle: Plenty of water to drink, green foods and protein included in a daily diet, sleeping during the night as much as possible for 7–8 hours, and getting some fresh air and exercise regularly can be crucial for concentration and focus.

# A wandering mind can be an unhappy mind

- Concentration is difficult because there is so much going on inside and outside us.

- In this digital age there are so many competing demands on our attention it is **hard to focus our thoughts.**

- Attention focuses on and **absorbs what it rests on.**

- What it repeatedly rests on can **influence our intuitions, thoughts, and actions**.

- Our minds do **tend to wander towards negative** content and negative experiences.

- **Thoughts can overwhelm us and trigger emotions** and more thoughts, for instance remembering an argument or a difficult meeting can stir up emotions that distract us still further.

- We **do not acknowledge the positive aspects of life as much** which leads to more negative thoughts.

- However, **we can train our minds** to recognize this trait, halt the process, and direct our thoughts in a more positive direction with **self-talk.**

## Self-talk

- A form of concentration training because you have to **focus on the words.**

- **Self-talk changes your mindset** and identity; if you repeat certain words they go inside and rewire your brain to act out what the words describe. For example, **'I am excellent at concentrating'** or **'I have a good memory'**.

- It is important to **make your statement in the present tense**, as though it is happening now.

- Your **brain starts to believe it** then and works towards that outcome (Knight, 2019).

## Manage distractions

- **Stay away from your phone** (and social media and emails) when you need to concentrate. Put it in another room for a while or turn it to airplane mode.

- Your concentration will improve if you can **train your brain to refrain from attending to distractions** for longer and longer periods.

- Keep your **workspace tidy.**

- **Link study to small rewards**, a piece of chocolate or an outing, to build positive associations.

- **Break up tasks** into small, manageable units.

- Consider when your **most productive time of day is** (when you feel most energetic and focused).

- Work in **blocks of time.**

- If all else fails, try a **distraction free zone! Take yourself away from your usual environment** and go to the library or even a coffee shop and take what you need to complete your work. You might complete in 1 hour what would have taken 2–3 hours in your own space because you are free from the usual distractions.

A student told us

'Simply looking for "study music" on YouTube and listening with headphones can help you block out distractions and focus on studying.'

## Mindfulness is really attention training

- Mindfulness strengthens the focus area of your brain and can therefore lead to higher grades.

- There are **many benefits** associated with mindfulness **for both physical and mental health**, especially when undertaken with an attitude of kindness, patience, and gentleness.

- It can **slow down thoughts** and **smooth emotions.**

- You can use the exercise below to calm yourself, reduce anxiety, and increase concentration on your academic work.

- Regulating attention leads to becoming more self-aware, building new neurons, and reinforcing the pathways in the brain.

- This leads to putting life and events into perspective.

- A sense of wholeness develops over time with mindfulness.

## Mindfulness exercise

1. Sit or lie down quietly and let yourself feel still.
2. Concentrate on your breathing and the rise and fall of your stomach.
3. Every time your thoughts invade your head bring your attention back to your breathing.
4. Do not get angry or frustrated by your thoughts – acknowledge them and let them float by.
5. Visualizing an image such as a shape, a number, or a symbol or saying a mantra such as 'my mind and body are calm' can be an alternative to concentrating on breathing. Keep bringing your mind back from your thoughts to whatever works best.

6. With time and practice you will find that there will be longer and longer periods of peace in your head. Even one minute is good to start with!

7. This peace will ultimately spread into other areas of your life and help you to concentrate on your academic work, among other things, for longer and longer periods of time.

> 'Having the right amount and quality of sleep helps improve energy levels, focus, motivation, and mood.'

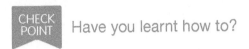

Tick the boxes. Revisit these sections if not.

☐ Improve your focus?

☐ Be more aware of the impact of your thoughts and emotions?

☐ Use self-talk?

☐ Manage distractions?

☐ Try a concentration exercise?

☐ Consider the impact of your lifestyle on your studies?

# How can I use
# my strengths for
# academic success?

10 second
summary

Reflecting on your strengths can be
used to support any weaknesses.
Implementing proven strategies can
help the dyslexic student to use their
strengths to work smart.

60 second
summary

## To work smart you need to think sharp

To think sharp you need to be aware of and understand:

- Your own thinking and way of learning.

- Some general patterns of human thinking and behaviour.

- The ability of the brain to change and grow throughout the duration of our lives.

- Your strengths in a world that is crying out for your skills.

- That dyslexic students often have an aptitude for sharp thinking: they do it anyway, they are naturals!

- Metacognition, embracing failure, having a growth mindset, counterintuitive thinking, and the benefits of perseverance as these will have a positive impact on your academic studies.

# What influences working smart?

To work smart you need to critically examine your approach to life:

- Are you aware of your beliefs?

- Do you leave time for reflection?

- Do you examine your responses?

- Do you consider your behaviour?

- Do you question your thinking?

- Are you persistent?

Working smart To work smart you need to understand your own way of learning and thinking. You need to understand your strengths and differences and know of and use strategies that reinforce the natural tendencies of those with dyslexia to see connections and patterns, to think visually, and see solutions where others do not.

## Metacognition

- Metacognition is the 'confidence and the ability **to think about our thinking while we think, changing it where it needs to be changed**. It means conscious self-reflection and monitoring' (Flavell, 1979: 80).

- Metacognition is relevant in every aspect of our lives.

Metacognition Critically analysing and reflecting on the way you think and learn. This information can then be used to monitor progress and make changes, where appropriate, in your behaviour or the approach to a task to improve the outcome.

## Metacognition in practice

- When you complete **a task and it doesn't go as planned** take some time to think about the reasons **why.**

- Dismiss negative thinking. **Collect feedback, reflect, and input any new data** from this process into future actions.

- Has this improved the results?

- What have you learnt?

- This process is a **highly effective way of doing things more efficiently** and achieving successful outcomes.

| Problem | Negative thought | Positive potential actions |
|---|---|---|
| I got very low marks for my essay. Tutor feedback: poor structure. | I'm terrible at essays. | Look at some essay planning tips regarding structure. Plan essay in a 'big picture' way using mind maps or an essay planner. Seek advice from tutor. Look at good essay models. |
| My mind goes blank in exams. | I've got a bad memory and I'm going to fail. | Use positive self-talk. How can you revise more effectively next time? Understand the material so you do not rote learn for exams. Build up your mindfulness practice. |
| I'm always late with work submissions and appointments. | I can't do anything about it. There is something wrong with me. | Get a large planner on your wall and use post-it notes to move information around. Input deadlines and appointments. Sync with your online calendars and diaries. Use reminder facilities. Tackle procrastination. |

Using metacognition to improve an outcome

Can you think of some situations where you could use metacognition to improve an outcome? Add these into the table below.

| Problem | Response | Positive potential actions |
|---------|----------|----------------------------|
|         |          |                            |
|         |          |                            |
|         |          |                            |

A student
told us

'It is good to be aware of your strengths because focusing on areas in which you do well could effectively be the difference between two grades.'

## Failure

- Failure is **not a tragedy** as we are often led to believe as children.

- **Failure is a human learning tool** and **a stepping stone to success.**

- Joshua R. Eyler, in his book *How humans learn* (2018: 174), states that **'the brains of human beings are designed to detect and to learn from failure.'**

- Not only do we learn valuable lessons from failure but **our brains grow and change from these experiences**, new neurons are made, and their pathways reinforced.

## Growth mindset

- Carol Dweck in her research found that those who believed in the **plasticity of the brain or 'growth mindset'** (Dweck, 2006) achieved **more success** in many different areas of life than those with a more 'fixed mindset'.

- A growth mindset is based on the belief that you **can change your brain through your own efforts**.

- Further research by Dweck has shown that **adopting a growth mindset** has resulted in an **increase in students' academic performance**.

**An example of mindset** is well illustrated in Richard Wiseman's book *The luck factor: The scientific study of the lucky mind* (2004).

In an experiment carried out by Wiseman to establish what made people 'lucky' or 'unlucky', he asked a group to read a newspaper and count the photographs. Within that paper were two half page ads; one stated that there were 54 photographs in the paper and the other that if you saw the ad you would be given £100. The 'lucky' people saw the ads and the 'unlucky' tended not to. Wiseman concluded that there was no fundamental difference between 'lucky' and 'unlucky people', it was their mindset that separated them. The good news was that once 'unlucky' people were made aware of this and widened their perspective, they could become 'lucky' people!

## Counter-intuitive thinking

Bryan Greetham in his book *Smart thinking* (2016) suggests **we make judgements and decisions without being consciously aware** of how or why we made them.

- We **often rely on our intuitions**, which can be biased and not based on evidence.

- He says that **counter-intuitive thinking**, where we **suspend our beliefs** and replace our intuitive thinking with a slower, **more analytical and reflective type of thinking** can **generate new, interesting, and different perspectives.**

A bat and ball cost £1.10

The bat costs £1.00 more than the ball

How much does the ball cost?

Generally, our first thought is that the ball costs 10p but this is not the case: the bat costs £1 **more** than the ball – so think again!

Answer at end of section.

## Working smart leads to

- Independence in learning.

- The ability to stand out from the crowd.

- Enhanced creative thinking and problem-solving skills.

- Academic and workplace success.

- Improved employability chances.

- Increased self-esteem and confidence.

- Reduced stress and anxiety.

## Impact on academic studies

The dyslexic brain according to Eide and Eide (2011) has: 'the ability to perceive relationships like analogies, metaphors, paradoxes, similarities, differences, implications, gaps and imbalances' (p.5) and to 'unite all kinds of information about a particular object or thought into a single global or big picture view' (p.84).

Students with dyslexia can excel at being curious, creative, and seeing connections where others don't (Wallbank, 2018).

- The dyslexic brain can be very good at making new connections between two old ideas and coming up with a new one, which can be very useful in assignments.

- Your presentations will be more interesting and convincing.

- Your writing will be more perceptive and unique because you will have made the ideas your own.

- You will learn 'how' to think not just 'what' to think.

- Persevere and you will see problems and solutions from a different perspective.

> 'See setbacks as learning opportunities and if at first you don't succeed, keep trying.'

Metacognition mapping

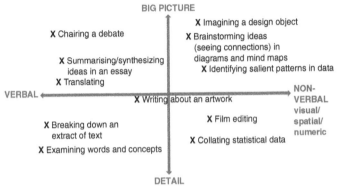

**Figure 9.1** Big picture/detail qualities

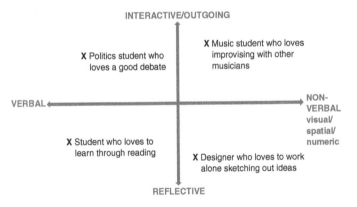

**Figure 9.2** Outgoing/reflective qualities

Now try and plot your qualities in the maps below.

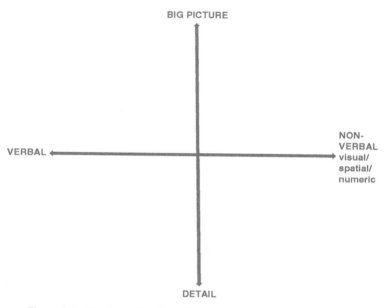

**Figure 9.3** Big picture/detail qualities template

(Klein, 2016)

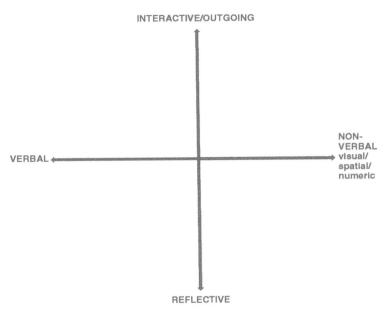

**Figure 9.4** Outgoing/reflective qualities template

(Klein, 2016)

Answer to counter-intuitive thinking question: ball costs 5p, bat £1.05.

# Final checklist: How to know you are done

☐ Do you now know that **dyslexia need not hold you back in any area of life**? In fact, it has some very useful strengths!

☐ Do you understand why **time management is key to academic success**?

☐ Will you use some strategies like the **urgent/important matrix** to prioritize your tasks?

☐ Do you think that you might be able to **tackle procrastination now** you know more about it and have learnt a few strategies?

☐ Do you understand the importance of **preview** or getting the big picture?

☐ Do you remember that **reading** (and even going through lecture slides) **four times more quickly rather than once slowly** will help you read faster and absorb more information?

☐ Will you **review** information within 24 hours and then skim periodically afterwards to help you forget less?

☐ Can you be creative with **imagination and association to help you remember** more?

☐ Can you see that **mapping might support your academic work** and **help with making connections** that you might not have seen in a linear format?

☐ Will you try **positive self-talk** and **mindfulness** to improve concentration?

☐ **Reflect on the activities you have completed in this book.** Reflect on how you complete tasks and how you can use that knowledge to influence future tasks and **improve your performance.**

☐ Do you understand that **the way you live in terms of sleep, nutrition, and exercise is closely linked to academic performance**?

# Glossary

**Academic procrastination**  Students who put off academic work which they know they should be starting (Tefula, 2014).

**Big picture**  Getting the big picture is to briefly look at the whole of the information in front of you, e.g., book, article, lecture slides, and see the extent of it to the boundaries. It helps you to identify the main points and to slot-in the detail more easily to the whole.

**Chunking time**  Breaking study time into 25–40 minute study sessions with a 5–10 minute break before starting the next period of study. The breaks are as important as the study sessions.

**Metacognition**  Critically analysing and reflecting on the way you think and learn. This information can then be used to monitor progress and make changes, where appropriate, in your behaviour or the approach to a task to improve the outcome.

**Mindfulness**  The art of being able to distance yourself from your thoughts and let them move by without being affected by them. It is a form of brain training and can help focus, which can then improve your grades and reduce anxiety. To develop mindfulness takes practice and persistence but can have big rewards.

**Mindset**  How you set your mind and your beliefs. Students with a 'growth' mindset (Dweck, 2006), who believe that the brain can grow and change with learning, tend to perform better than students with a 'fixed' mindset. Thinking about a task before you do it can get you in the right mindset and make the task easier.

**Mind mapping**  A diagrammatic, visual way of portraying and analysing information using trigger words and images that encourage the left and right sides of the brain to work together to reinforce memories. Useful for planning, taking/making notes, and revision, etc. Shows the big picture and how ideas are connected. Clarifies thinking and simplifies complex ideas. An effective memory tool. Encourages creative thinking, which promotes more ideas.

**Neuro-diversity**  The view that any brain differences are normal and not deficits. Neuro-diverse people are unique in the way they interact with and interpret the world. The strengths of people with any learning difference are acknowledged and valued.

**Preview**  Similar to getting the big picture; skim and scan something quickly before looking at it more closely. You can identify how the parts fit together then and what you need to concentrate on.

**Recall**  Retrieval or recall deals with getting the information out of the mind and is one of the best ways to reinforce memory. The more you practice retrieval the more it motivates your mind to commit new information to memory.

**Reflection**  Taking a few minutes to review what has been learned in a recent class or study experience and asking yourself questions such as: 'What went well?' and 'What could've gone better?'.

**Review**  In this context, review is to skim or look back over a book, study period, lecture slides, a lecture, or tutorial to help to embed the information.

**Self-talk**  Short sentences repeated internally or externally until your brain starts to believe them and then works towards that outcome (Knight, 2019). Self-talk is also a form of concentration training because you have to focus on the words. It changes your mindset and identity.

**Visualization**  Link words to images in your mind to remember more. We are visual beings so we can use our imagination to create mental pictures to help embed memories.

**Working smart**  To work smart you need to understand your own way of learning and thinking. You need to understand your strengths and differences and know of and use strategies that reinforce the natural tendencies of those with dyslexia to see connections and patterns, to think visually, and see solutions where others do not.

# Next steps

**Made by Dyslexia:** www.madebydyslexia.org

A charity involving Richard Branson and other successful people and celebrities who feel that they and their contributions to the world have been 'made' by their dyslexia.

**British Dyslexia Association:** www.bda-dyslexia.org.uk

**Check out Assistive Technology (AT), it can level the playing field for students with dyslexia.**

Investigate free supportive AT. Some paid AT can be particularly useful and is worth the cost. It's surprising what is out there and AT is on the increase and does evolve so it is good to carry out your own research and ask around. There are pens that record and pens that read aloud the words they trace over.

# Microsoft accessibility features

**Microsoft** have some very useful free **in-built support features** within Office 365 and Teams, such as:

- **Immersive Reader** (reading words out loud and highlighting them as it does so, which is very good for focus and memory. There are apps that do this too and combine highlighting and note-taking facilities).

- **Dictate** (a speech to text facility).

- The ability to **change your background colour** (this is helpful to reduce glare for anyone with visual sensitivities and can make reading easier).

Other platforms will have in-built features too that many people do not know about.

# References and further reading

Abbasi, I.S. & Alghamdi, N.G. (2015). The prevalence, predictors, causes, treatment, and implications of procrastination behaviours in general, academic, and work setting. *International Journal of Psychological Studies*, 7(1).

Allum, L. Minns, N. & Szumko, J. (2016). The 'Metacognitive Mind Map'. *Journal of Neurodiversity in Higher Education*, 2: 59–75. Available from adshe.org.uk.

Awan, S. (2018). *A Study of academic procrastination*. Buckingham, UK: Psychology Department, University of Buckingham.

Balkis, M. & Duru, E. (2007). The evaluation of the major characteristics and aspects of the procrastination in the framework of psychological counseling and guidance. *Educational Sciences: Theory & Practice*, 7(1): 376–385.

Buzan, T. (2011). *Buzan's study skills*. Harlow: BBC Active.

Brunswick, N. (2012). *Supporting Dyslexic Adults in Higher Education and the Workplace*. Malden, MA: Wiley-Blackwell.

Chatfield, T. (2019). *Think critically.* London: SAGE.

Connerr, H. (2016). *Fish can't climb trees: Capitalize on your brain's unique wiring to improve the way you learn and communicate.* London: Watkins.

de Charms, R. (1968). *Personal causation: The internal affective determinants of behaviour.* New York: Academic Press.

Dweck, C. (2006). *Mindset.* New York: Random House.

Eide, B.L. & Eide, F.F. (2011). *Unlocking the hidden potential of the dyslexic brain.* London: Hay House.

Eyler, R. (2018). *How humans learn: The science and stories behind effective college teaching.* Morgantown: West Virginia University Press.

*Farther and Sun: A Dyslexic Road Trip* (2018), BBC Four, 2019.

Ferrari, J.R. & Díaz-Morales, J. F. (2014). Procrastination and mental health coping: A brief report related to students. *Individual Differences Research*, 12(1): 8–11.

Ferrari, J.R., O'Callaghan, J. & Newbegin, I. (2005). Prevalence of procrastination in the United States, United Kingdom, and Australia: arousal and avoidance delays among adults. *North American Journal of Psychology*, 7(1).

Flavell, J. H. (1979). Metacognition and cognitive monitoring: A new era of cognitive-developmental inquiry. *American Psychologist*, 34: 80.

Godwin, J. (2012). *Studying with Dyslexia.* Basingstoke: Palgrave MacMillan.

Greetham, B. (2016). *Smart thinking: How to think conceptually, design solutions and make decisions.* New York: Palgrave MacMillan.

Gupta, R., Hershey, D. & Gaur, J. (2012). Time perspective and procrastination in the workplace: An empirical investigation. *Current Psychology*, 31(2): 195–211.

Klein, S. (2016). *Metacognition mapping*. Available from adshe.org.uk.

Knight, K. (2012). *Mind mapping*. MindLily.

Knight, K. (2016). *Triple your reading, memory and concentration*. MindLily.

Knight, K. (2019). *Concentration*. MindLily.

Knight, K. (2021). *Everyday memory*. MindLily.

National Working Party on Dyslexia (1999). *Dyslexia in higher education: policy, provision and practice*. Hull, UK: Psychology Department, University of Hull.

Nichols, S.A., McLeod, J.S. and McLeod, H.S.T. (2009). Screening for dyslexia, dyspraxia and Meares-IRLEN syndrome in Higher Education. *Dyslexia*, 15(1): 42–60.

Redway, K. (2000). *Beat the bumf!: cut clutter, read rapidly and succeed in the information jungle*. Cirencester: Management Books.

Reid, G. and Fawcett, A. (2008). *The Sage Handbook of Dyslexia*. Washington, DC: SAGE.

Rozental, A. & Carlbring, P. (2013). Internet-based cognitive behavior therapy for procrastination: Study protocol for a randomized controlled trial. *Journal of Medical Internet Research*, 15(11): 27.

Rush, D. (2020). *Build your argument*. London: SAGE.

Ryan, R.M. & Deci, E.L. (2000). Intrinsic and extrinsic motivations: Classic definitions and new directions, *Contemporary Educational Psychology* 25: 54–67.

Senécal, C., Koestner, R. & Vallerand, R.J., (1995). Self-regulation and academic procrastination. *The Journal of Social Psychology*, 135(5): 607–619.

Singleton, C. (2004). Using computer-based assessment to identify learning problems. In L. Florian & J. Hegarty (Eds.), *ICT and Special Educational Needs* (pp. 46–63). Milton Keynes: Open University Press.

Sirois, F. M., Melia-Gordon, M. L., & Pychyl, T. A. (2003). "I'll look after my health, later": An investigation of procrastination and health. *Personality and Individual Differences*, 35(5): 1167–1184.

Snowling, M.J. (2019). *Dyslexia: A very short introduction*. Oxford: Oxford University Press.

Shon, P.C. (2019*). Plan your essay*. London: SAGE.

Steel, P. (2007). The nature of procrastination: A meta-analytic and theoretical review of quintessential self-regulatory failure. *Psychological Bulletin*, 133(1): 65–94.

Svartdal, F. & Steel, P. (2017). Irrational delay revisited: Examining five procrastination scales in a global sample. *Frontiers in Psychology*, 8.

Tefula, M. (2012). *How to get a First: Insights and advice from a first-class graduate*. Basingstoke: Palgrave Macmillan.

Tefula, M. (2014). *Student procrastination: Seize the day and get more work done*. Basingstoke: Palgrave Macmillan.

Tice, D. M., & Baumeister, R. F. (1997). Longitudinal study of procrastination, performance, stress and health: The costs and benefits of dawdling. *Psychological Science*, 8(6): 454–458.

Wallbank, A.J. (2018). *Academic writing and dyslexia: A visual guide to writing at university*. Abingdon: Routledge.

Wiseman, R. (2004). *The luck factor, the scientific study of the lucky mind*. London: Arrow Books.